IDEA WISE Basements & Attics

Inspiration & Information for the Do-It-Yourselfer

Matthew Paymar

Creative Publishing
international

CHANHASSEN, MINNESOTA
www.creativepub.com

Creative Publishing international

Copyright © 2006
Creative Publishing international, Inc.
18705 Lake Drive East
Chanhassen, Minnesota 55317
1-800-328-3895
www.creativepub.com
All rights reserved

Printed in China

10 9 8 7 6 5 4 3 2 1

President/CEO: Ken Fund
Vice President/Publisher: Linda Ball
Vice President/Retail Sales & Marketing: Kevin Haas

Executive Editor: Bryan Trandem
Creative Director: Tim Himsel
Managing Editor: Tracy Stanley

Author: Matthew Paymar
Editor: Thomas Lemmer
Senior Art Director: Dave Schelitzche
Photo Editor: Julie Caruso
Book Designer: Kari Johnston
Technical Illustrator: Earl Slack
Production Manager: Linda Halls

IdeaWise: Basements & Attics

Library of Congress Cataloging-in-Publication Data

Paymar, Matthew.
  Ideawise basements and attics :
inspiration & information for the
do-it-yourselfer / Matthew Paymar.
    p. cm.
  Includes index.
  ISBN 1-58923-224-0 (soft cover)
  1. Basements--Remodeling--Amateurs' manuals.
  2. Do-it-yourself work.
  I. Title: Basements and attics. II. Title.
  TH4816.3.B35P39 2006
  643'.5--dc22
                                        2005019606

Table of Contents

Introduction

If you feel as though you could use some extra living space, you're not alone. According to a recent survey by the National Association of Homebuilders, the median size of our current home's finished living space is 1770 square feet, but we would prefer a minimum of 2000 square feet. And homebuilders are responding: Homes built today average over 2200 square feet of finished living space. However, if you don't have the luxury to build a larger home or have an addition built, an unfinished or underutilized attic or basement offers a world of tantalizing possibilities.

We demand more today from our homes than ever before. In the past, it was sufficient to have a kitchen, one bath, a couple bedrooms, a dining area and some living space. Today, however, we expect to have specialized spaces for a variety of activities and pursuits that either didn't exist in the not-so-distant past, like home theaters, or weren't very often located in the home, like today's home offices. In addition, many leisure activities have been relocated to the home, creating a demand for specialized spaces such as hobby rooms, game rooms, exercise rooms, and spas.

So where can you find more space in your existing home? The answer is literally right below your feet and right above your head, in your basement and attic.

Historically, basements and attics have been pragmatic spaces. Basements are far more common in colder climates than in warmer ones, due to the fact that they create an insulating air barrier that makes the house easier to heat in the winter. In areas where the water table is too high, there are no basements.

Attics, too, have been a matter of practicality, often determined by the weather. The amount of rainfall typical for an area often determined the roof pitch of the houses built there, and the attics were simply the byproducts of the roof design. In arid climates, many homes have flat roofs and, consequently, no attic space.

Over half of all houses in North America are more than 30 years old. Many of these attics and basements are still dramatically underutilized spaces. Many are just empty shoeboxes, or, at best, cluttered storerooms. Even in new construction, attics and basements often are left unfinished so that the new homeowner can determine for her- or himself how best to incorporate the space.

Any room can be moved to an attic or basement. There are advantages and disadvantages to each location, depending upon the intended needs or usage for the space. We'll address those concerns as they arise in each chapter. But if you know you want to convert unfinish basements and attics into living spaces, there are three main considerations: zoning and building limitations, economics, and design preferences.

Many neighborhoods are regulated by strict zoning ordinances that either prohibit expansion of a home's existing footprint or make the process of adding to a home a nightmare. In most cases, looking toward your basement or attic is your best option.

While there are zoning regulations that apply to basements and attics as well, they are primarily related to safety and to the suitability of the space for conversion. For example, because there is a difference between "active" and "inactive" weight, the regulations governing the size, spacing and span of floor joists are stricter for habitable space than for storage space. Other regulations pertain more to comfort: With few exceptions, habitable rooms, must have a minimum 70 square feet of floor space and at least a 7-ft. ceiling.

For the most part, zoning regulations pertaining to basements and attics are ones you'd like to follow anyway. Make sure to work with your local building department to ensure that your basement or attic meets local building code requirements.

For most of us, our homes are the single biggest investment of our lives. However, we have to think about this investment not only in terms of finances, but also in terms of the labor, time, and care invested in making a house a home.

Remodeling a basement or attic can be accomplished for a fraction of the cost of building an addition. Additions not only require a new foundation, but they also involve erecting an entirely new structure. On the other hand, basements and attics are already enclosed, framed and roofed, and the services are already wired and plumbed into the walls. In fact, it typically costs 50% less to refinish your basement and attic than to construct an addition.

For many, the most rewarding and fun part of any remodel is planning the initial design. At this stage in the process, play with any idea that suits your fancy. Have fun with it. There will come a time when budgets and schedules limit what is possible, but in the beginning, allow yourself to imagine anything you want. You may find that a detail that seemed too indulgent at first becomes so important to you that you are able to find a way to make it work.

Because basements and attics are separate from the rest of the house, the design does not necessarily have to respond to the thematic elements found on the main floors. You could choose to create a consistent aesthetic throughout the house, but you're also free to be more adventurous or even whimsical with these spaces. Remember: It's your own unique needs, interests, and lifestyle that will transform an unused basement and attic into the useful spaces you're after.

How to Use This Book

The pages of *IdeaWise Basements and Attics* are packed with images of interesting, attractive, efficient basements and attics. And although we hope you enjoy looking at them, they're more than pretty pictures: they're inspiration accompanied by descriptions, facts, and details meant to help you plan your basement or attic project wisely.

Some of the basements and attics you see here will suit your sense of style, while others may not appeal to you at all. If you're serious about finishing or remodeling these often underused spaces in your home, read every page—there's as much to learn in what you don't like as in what you do. Look at each photograph carefully and take notes. The details you gather are the seeds from which ideas for your new basement or attic will sprout.

IdeaWise Basements and Attics contains six chapters: Family Spaces, Home Offices, Hobby Spaces, Rec Rooms, Bedrooms, and In-law Suites. In each chapter, you'll find several features, each of which contains a specific type of wisdom.

DesignWise features hints and tips—insider tricks—from professional designers, architects, and/or builders. Special thanks to Jake Schoegel, Peter Feinmann, Rosemary McMonigal, Michael Anschel, and Robert Gerloff.

DollarWise describes money-saving ideas that can be adapted to your own plans and circumstances.

IdeaWise illustrates a clever do-it-yourself project for each topic.

Some chapters also include Words to the Wise, a glossary of terms that may not be familiar to you.

Another important feature of IdeaWise Basements and Attics is the Resource Guide on pages 134 to 141. The Resource Guide contains as much information as possible about the spaces showcased in this book, including contact information for designers and manufacturers, when available.

CHAPTER 1

Family Spaces

Family spaces are all-purpose, casual living spaces where the entire family can gather together to relax. They should be comfortable, practical additions that family members find themselves naturally gravitating towards during the evening. They should to be open and inviting, yet intimate environments that encourages familial interaction. And basements and attics are prime locations for such needs.

Family spaces tend to be added to basements rather than attics for three reasons. First, the preferred size for a family room is 12 sq. ft. × 16 sq. ft., and basements are more likely to offer this much space. Secondly, basements tend to be darker than attics, an attribute conducive to watching movies and television. And finally, in more ambitious family spaces that include laundry rooms, bathrooms or wet bars, it is usually easier to connect to the existing plumbing in basements.

Whether you're planning a modest remodel or something more lavish, take heart in the fact that, on average, over 80% of the costs of creating a new family space are recovered in an increase in your home's value.

Family Rooms

Family rooms are among the easiest and least expensive ways to add finished living space to your home because they do not require an egress window, a closet, new plumbing, or other specialized features. In fact, other than offering at least one quiet and comfortable conversation area with comfortable seating, there is no single definition of a family room.

There are some recurring themes to many family rooms, however. For instance, it's a good idea to have a focal point in the room, such as a fireplace, gas stove or media center. Built-in storage is also a common feature. Cabinets, shelving and drawers often house the video, music, and gaming equipment and help keep books, magazines, and other media organized.

The frosted glass lets in light from windows in the exercise room even when doors are closed.

This family room offers the best of two worlds:

Comfy chairs with task lighting are oriented around a gas fireplace with a poured concrete hearth, oak mantle, and slate stone tile to create a peaceful space to read or talk. At the same time, the built-in maple cabinets house the entertainment system and media storage for a more lively setting.

Drain tiles around the house perimeter and a sump pump keeps the basement dry enough for carpeting.

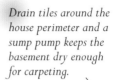

Defining spaces without the use of walls is a common problem in basement remodels. The decorative slate tile accents not only repeat the materials found in the fireplace, they create a threshold that helps to distinguish between the game area and family room. The effect was achieved simply by furring out the wall with 2 × 4s. Other design strategies have also been employed to define space: The chandelier is the centerpiece of the game area and the lounge chair in foreground signals the beginning of the family room.

Slate stone tiles are cut in a variety of nonstandard sizes for interest.

In family rooms with an entertainment center, creating appropriate storage for your audio/visual equipment and media is a major concern. At the low end there are ready-to-assemble (RTA) modular shelving systems or manufactured stand-alone units that can meet your basic needs. Many of these options, however, are disappointing to style-conscious consumers.

In this basement, a large custom built-in provides the perfect backdrop for this homeowner's entertainment center—keeping all wires out of sight and everything organized and within reach. The cabinet doors hiding the TV are on a pivot door slide so they can slide back out of the way when in use. Together, the alder wainscot paneling, backlit storage cabinets, and array of wall sconces bring a richness and warmth to what used to be a dark lower level.

Words to the Wise

A good lighting plan is important in any room, but it is critical in a basement where the presence of fewer windows result in a greater reliance on artificial lighting

- **Ambient or general light** is the soft, diffuse, indirect natural or artificial light in a room that contributes to the overall mood (e.g., wall sconces).

- Ceiling fixtures produce **downlighting** (e.g., pendant, recessed, and track lights).

- **Task lighting** is directed to a specific area to help you perform a task (e.g., table lamps, under-counter fixtures, and spotlights).

- **Accent lighting** is directed to a specific area to illuminate a decorative element or space (e.g., art light).

Fireplaces have a strong, positive effect on a home's selling price, increasing resale value by an average of 13%.

Benches double as storage for firewood or media.

The rustic fireplace outfitted with old Chicago brick, a thick mantel, and alder paneling matching the built-in on the other wall, provides an alternative focal point to the room. The surround seating creates an intimate conversation or reading area when the television is behind closed doors.

This elegant family room is the perfect space to relax by the warmth of a fire or the glow of the big screen television. However, the real feature of this room is the full wall that has been crafted to create the feeling you're in looking out onto the Italian countryside. The texture and appeal of the stone archway and pillars framing the painting is repeated in the tile of the fireplace surround, as well as in the arches and moldings at the entranceways.

Warm, neutral colors, faux finishes, and columns with molding styles matching the upstairs give a Mediterranean feel to this lower level. A beautiful curved, granite top bar adds to the relaxed atmosphere. The bar has ample seating along the front for entertaining and is equipped with a full-sized refrigerator, microwave, dishwasher, oven, and cooktop.

Mirrors make a space seem bigger and enliven "dead" areas on smaller walls.

A bank of windows creates a steady block of natural light in an otherwise dark corner.

Family rooms don't have to be in the basement. An attic can be made into a spectacular family room just as comfortable for family gatherings as any basement. However, the vaulted ceilings, odd corners and recesses, and smaller footprint can present a few design challenges.

Whatever the circumstances, just make sure that your attic provides at least 110 square ft. of habitable space and a ceiling clearance of at least 7-ft. 6-in., the minimum requirements for a family room set by the U.S. Department of Housing and Urban Development.

While high gable ceilings can be dramatic, they pose a design challenge in that they can make a room feel impersonal and intimidating. Lowered ceilings can help create spaces that are more interesting and less imposing. Even the suggestion of a lowered ceiling with the use of chandeliers, beams, archways or even terraces can make a significant difference.

In this case, a the seating area for the media room is tucked into a dormer and defined by the chandelier and the red oak hammer beam trusses. The spaces beneath a lowered feature will inevitably feel more private and comfortable than the rest of the attic.

A skylight brings soft ambient light into a cavernous space.

Dormers can be added to any attic to provide additional light and ventilation, or more importantly, to increase the available headroom and floor area to make room for a stairway, bathroom, or more habitable living space.

The sitting area takes advantage of the morning and afternoon sun. From the two window seats, there is a great view of a creek or the neighbor's expansive gardens. Double-hung windows take full advantage of the tall end wall.

Tudor-inspired finials soften the harsh corner created by the intersection of two beams.

FAMILY SPACES

This beautiful attic is organized into two cozy sitting areas around a sizeable earth-tone fireplace near the center of the room. What might otherwise be an intimidating attic, due to the tall walls and vaulted ceiling, is divided into more manageable, human-scale spaces.

Every element is well considered to create the bright, contemporary look of this family space. The skylights are aligned with the windows below to create a measured sense of rhythm in the repetition of shapes. These simple, linear lines are then repeated in the modern Scandinavian furniture. The variegated oak floor presents the only "pattern" in the room. It creates a sense of warmth and continuity, whereas a floor in a solid color would be monotonous in this already understated space. A circular wall hanging presents an interesting contrast to the straight lines in the room.

Light-colored painted walls & ceilings maximize brightness.

Bookshelves built into a wall provide storage without taking up floor space.

Vivid colors are making a comeback in interior design. In fact, in many rooms, the color story can be the main attraction. This is particularly true of basements and attics, where limited space sometimes dictates sparse décor. Clever use of color can cheer up a gloomy basement or make sense of the awkward angles in an attic.

Yellow ceiling fixtures create an eye-popping contrast to the complementary blue of the bar.

This curved row of recessed lighting illuminates the hallway and highlights wall color.

Keep baseboards simple in a room with low ceilings; elaborate molding can visually shorten a room.

A formerly long and narrow "bowling-alley" basement has been transformed into a vibrant lower level through the use of a few simple design principles. Most critically, the bar is placed in the center of the room rather than at the end or off to the side. This not only breaks up the space, but conceals exercise and storage areas behind the bar. The rounded wall on the left, which hides mechanicals as well as a bathroom and guest bedroom, softly pinches the long narrow room into two distinct sections.

The deep indigo blue of the bar and ceiling articulation (a 2"-deep decorative soffit) and rich Chinese red of the wall draw attention to these features because they are strong, saturated primary colors that play off one another well. The white ceiling, neutral carpeting and wall color, and blonde maple bar front and baseboards reflect light and make the space brighter.

Color Theory

There are several Color Harmonies derived from the color wheel that can make the process of choosing colors less perplexing.

• MONOCHROMATIC (single color) color combinations are variations in lightness and saturation of a single color. Their use creates a subtle reiteration of a color theme.

• ANALOGOUS colors (related hues—e.g., red and red-orange) are adjacent to one another on the color wheel. The use of these kindred colors creates a harmonious and unified effect.

• COMPLEMENTARY colors (opposite hues - e.g., red and green) are directly opposite one another on the color wheel. Their use creates an eye-popping color contrast.

• SPLIT-COMPLEMENTARY colors are produced when a dominant color is opposite not its complementary color but the two colors adjacent to its complementary.

Their use creates the same high contrast as complementaries, but without the same degree of intensity.

• TRIADIC colors are three equally spaced colors on the color wheel (making an equilateral triangle— e.g., purple, green, orange). Their use creates a harmonious color richness and strong visual contrast.

• Four colors are in a TETRADIC or DOUBLE COMPLEMENTARY relation when two pairs of opposites on the color wheel create two sets of high-contrast colors (e.g., yellow-purple and orange-blue).

When choosing paint, it is helpful to know that paint swatches are organized by three principles:

• The more black present in a color, the darker its VALUE.

• The more white present in a color, the higher its BRIGHTNESS.

• The deeper, more vibrant a color is, the greater its COLOR SATURATION.

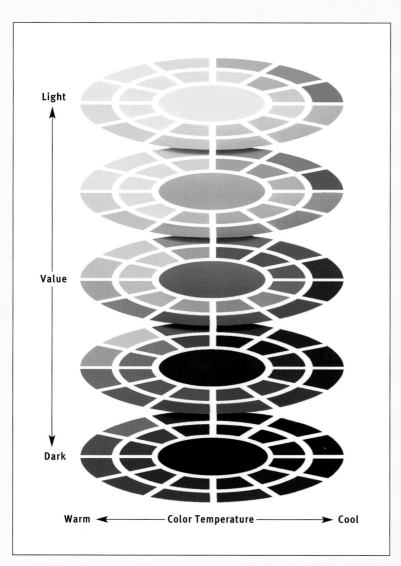

A vent in the laundry chute allows clothes to air out until released.

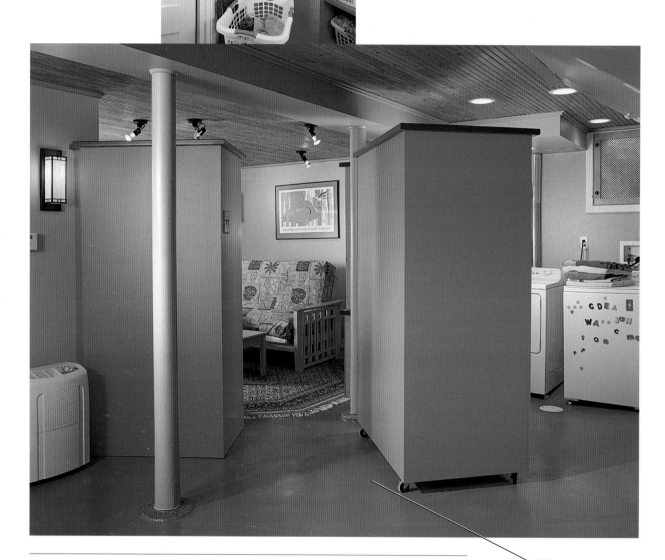

The challenge posed by this basement was how to separate the laundry room on the left from the adjacent family room without closing off this already small space with more walls. The ingenious solution comes in the form of custom storage shelving placed on wheels that can conceal the laundry area when not in use and be rolled out of the way when needed.

The powder blue support post and Granny Smith apple green wall are adjacent on the color wheel and together create a split-complementary color harmony with the opposing gypsy red of the shelving. This color relation further helps to visually separate the family room, laundry room, and hallway and yet create a smooth transition from one to the next.

In-floor radiant heating makes a concrete basement floor more comfortable.

The built-in oak shelving separates the laundry area from the family room, but because it doesn't extend all the way to the ceiling beam, it allows air to circulate and makes both areas feel a little less closed in. The lemon yellow wall shared by both rooms, and the bead board ceiling that complements the built-ins help to tie together the various spaces.

Spot lighting sheds light just where you need it.

The circuit panel is made part of the décor with a framed oak panel that matches the built-ins.

*Dollar*Wise

Although the initial purchase price of an Energy Star qualified light bulb is greater than an incandescent bulb, it is 75% more efficient. Using energy-efficient bulbs in just five of your more frequently used fixtures can save upwards of $60 a year in energy costs.

Gypsy red and Spanish gold are "analogous colors"—they are adjacent on the color wheel. Therefore, they are useful for defining separate areas in this basement without fighting with each other visually. A built-in fireplace makes this a cozy place to watch television while folding laundry. An adjoining game room on the left and full bathroom on the right provide other diversions while waiting for laundry cycles to end.

Because they are often narrow it is usually assumed that stairways should be painted a thin, light color. However, using rich or dark colors can create a sense of compression and then release that make the areas at the top or bottom of the stairs feel more expansive.

The grass green, royal blue, and lavender colors are arranged exactly as they appear on the color wheel. Both walls, then, are analogous colors to the steps, but have a dynamic relation to one another, making the stairwell an energetic area.

Just because the laundry room is utilitarian doesn't mean it has to be ugly. These stainless steel front-loading machines and grass green backdrop make the laundry area a visually interesting feature of the family room. Since the plumbing lines were already in place for the laundry area, it was easier to install an extra bath next door.

FAMILY SPACES

The absence of color can also be dramatic

By directing the eye upwards, vertical pine slats call attention to the cathedral ceiling.

South or west facing windows glow with natural light in the afternoon.

Colors don't need to be bold to make a strong impression. The superabundance of white in this room—from the walls to the built-in cabinetry to the ceiling to the sofas—maintains a fresh and tidy appearance. And with most everything put away in closed storage, the white surfaces draw attention to carefully placed display items and the room's detailed woodwork.

Home Theaters

The fastest growing trend in home design is the creation of a
Home Theater. Advances in flat screens, projectors, speakers,
and digital image and sound technology have made high-quality
home theater environments affordable to more people than
ever before. Home theaters, of course, can still cost hundreds
of thousands of dollars, but a good entry-level system including
a big screen (30" or larger) or projection television, a movie
playback device, speakers, and a surround sound capable
stereo receiver can be produced for under $5,000; a bare-
bones system can be assembled for as little as $2,000. The
space designed to maximize the potential of this technology
will add its own costs as well, but unlike the electronics,
the room itself will add value to your home at time of resale.

In most houses, the best location for a home theater is the
basement. This is because it is, obviously, much easier to
block out light in basements for a theater-like effect, but it's
also easier to insulate basements for sound than rooms on the
main floor. And after all, controlling light and sound is what
the home theater experience is all about.

*Front-projection televisions offer
the advantage of retractable
screens that disappear from view
when not in use.*

There are essentially three types of television screens in today's consumer market: the original direct view CRT (Cathrode Ray Tube) television, flat panels (e.g, LCD, plasma and new OLED monitors), and front- and rear-projection televisions.

They each have their advantages and disadvantages. The front-projection television shown here is unique, however, in that it is the only viewing option where you find yourself within the image environment rather than in front of it. In the industry, they say that the viewer is placed "inside the box" a condition which some argue offers the most intimate viewing experience of any home theater system.

Video projector technology, whether front or rear, comes in four styles: CRT (cathode ray tube), DLP (Digital Light Processing), LCD (Liquid Crystal Display), and the soon-to-be-obsolete LCOS (Liquid Crystal on Silicon).

Rear-projection televisions, like front projectors, form a small image and reflect it onto a screen. The receiver for a rear-projection television, however, is inside the viewing unit rather than across the room, so you do have to include some floor space for it in your design plan. Because the equipment is hidden inside cabinetry or walls, rear projectors have the advantage of minimizing the noise produced by its cooling fans.

In this home theater, a built-in cabinet doubles as a partition wall and bar, and separates the kitchen from the viewing area, while keeping snacks readily accessible.

Home theaters should be illuminated primarily with indirect lighting because soft ambient light doesn't create a distracting on-screen glare. Wall sconces that cast light upward toward the ceiling where it is diffused and reflected are ideal. Placing all lighting sources on dimmer switches is also a good idea because it provides more subtle control over lighting conditions.

Steel louvre shades protect windows and shield out all extraneous light, an important consideration in home theaters. All screen models can suffer from glare, but front-projection televisions in particular require a totally dark space or the image will appear washed out.

Sleek and stylish ergonomic seating with built-in cup-holders and footrest recliner keep you comfortable for extended viewing. The ideal seating arrangement should create a distance between the viewer and the television equal to 2 to 2.5 times the width of the screen.

*Design*Wise

Jake Schloegel, president
Schloegel Design Remodel, Inc.
Kansas City, MO

- Floors. Install tiered seating by framing an 8" floor on top of the existing floor and adding two or three risers. Add some concealed rope lighting in walkways so people can see in low lighting. Use carpet to help absorb some of the sound.

- Walls. Covering walls with sound-dampening material will significantly enhance sound quality. Some options include: wall carpeting, sound panels, quilts with fabric backing, and a new wallpaper made from super-thin cork material intended for this purpose.

- Lighting. Wall sconces along the side-walls are attractive and reproduce a theatre-like setting. Placing them on electronic dimmers that can coordinate with the start and finish of a movie will contribute to the effect.

- Seating. For maximum viewing comfort, use individual lounge chairs—ideally electronically controlled—that can adjust to the contours of each person's body. A variety of options are offered by companies that specialize in home theater seating.

- Style. Many of the great theaters were built during the time when Art Deco was at the height of its popularity. For a classic theater appearance, look in architectural salvage stores for accents from old movie houses including Art Deco doors, trim, and decorations.

This elegant screening room includes an adjacent bar with tasting table, and "refreshment stand." The curtains in front of the screen pull back by remote control. It's just like going to the theaters, only it's more convenient, more versatile, and the whole family gets free admission!

Clean sound transmission in a home theater is critical. The spaces between the overhead floor joists should be insulated with fiberglass, and the ceiling covered with drywall at least ½"-thick. One can also mount the drywall to resilient metal sound channels for extra insulation, or use an acoustical tile ceiling. Covering the walls with curtains or other room treatments such as corkboard will absorb sound reflections. Carpeting the floor also muffles sound.

The tiered, plush-velvet seating accented with down throw pillows is the very lap of luxury. A chandelier, hand-painted frescos, and walls made to look like aged plaster all contribute to the Tuscan design theme in this beautiful home theater.

The hand-painted mural in this ceiling inset is a bottom view of a duck pond.

*Idea*Wise

In small rooms where acoustics are important, it is essential that hard surfaces that reflect sound back to the listener be "dampened." To determine the most strategic locations for sound absorbing material (such as curtains, fabric wall coverings, or acoustic panels), sit in the listening position while an assistant moves a mirror along the sidewalls. When you can see the reflection of the speakers in the mirror, that's where you should provide for some absorption.

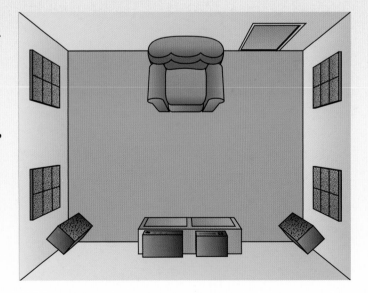

CHAPTER 2

Home Offices

Home offices are becoming a necessity for many of us: a 58% majority of all new homeowners request a home office. Some of us want a dedicated space just to manage daily tasks such as paying bills, surfing the Internet, and doing homework. However, there are a growing number of people who work income-generating jobs frequently or exclusively from their homes. In fact, nearly 20% of all working adults reported that they did at least some work at home as part of their primary job, according to the last survey conducted by the Bureau of Labor Statistics. And with computer technology growing by leaps and bounds daily, the number of telecommuters is only going to skyrocket.

Whatever your needs, basements and attics are great locations for a home office. They are generally quieter spaces than those on first or second floors, and their out-of-the-way location frees up traditionally defined living space in the rest of the house for everyday use. In order to be productive when working and relaxed when "at home," we need a sense of separation between our work-life and home-life. The act of descending or ascending the stairs to a basement or attic affords us this sense of departure from our normal home space and becomes a kind of "commute." The transition can help us enter the mindset necessary for whatever set of tasks awaits us at the bottom or top of the landing.

At their best, home offices provide a home away from home, where work itself becomes a retreat. Home offices can do more than simply provide space for traditionally defined work activities. A unique design can create an environment that makes going to work a pleasure.

A computer screen should be at or just below eye level with the keyboard at lap level.

Task lights should be 38" to 42" from the floor to shed enough light without creating a glare.

This homeowner has combined traditional cherry wood in furniture, flooring, and built-ins with a playful nautical theme to create a warm and inviting home office. Knotty pine-lined dormers suggest the shape of wooden-hulled ships pulling into port, and details such as the nautical-theme ceiling lighting fixture and the boat accent pieces are subtle touches that set the mood for the entire room. And of course, the nearby living room area provides space to socialize or take power naps for those much-needed breaks in the workday.

Windows in adjacent dormers create a pleasant cross breeze.

Words to the Wise

Rafters: are regularly spaced beams that slope from the ridge of a roof to the eaves. They compose the framing to which the roof decking is attached. Any attic with rafters that provide 7½ feet of headroom over 50% of the useable floor area is suitable for conversion.

Trusses: are prefabricated structural assemblies constructed with lumber and metal gusset plates. Trusses are designed to be stronger, lighter, and less expensive to install than rafters. However, trusses often leave too little room for an attic conversion, and the internal supports cannot be altered without seriously weakening the roof structure.

If you have the luxury of dedicating all or even a significant portion of your attic or basement to a home office, consider establishing multiple workstations. Devoting space to each of the specific tasks you perform in your office will keep you more organized and on-task. For instance, it may help clear your head to have one space for creative work such as writing, drafting, or design, and another for all home- and office-related administrative tasks.

Whitewashed pine planks create an attractive, functional and affordable attic floor.

Many people find that an L-shaped desk is a convenient space in which to work. A computer station as well as a writing and filing surface can both be accommodated with this arrangement. You should be about an arm's length away from the monitor screen when you're sitting back in the chair. Your eyes should be level with an imaginary line that is about 2 or 3 inches below the top of the monitor.

This gable extension provides a cozy, self-contained second workstation for the homeowner, who is a photographer, to sort through photographs. Just around the corner in the waiting room, an inexpensive bookcase was created with boards installed between the wall and a wood and plaster "chase" that hides a chimney and venting pipe, while the nearby narrow desk provides a great place to sort mail, jot notes, or set appointments—any of those small tasks that require space and time but that you wouldn't want taking over your main workspace.

This stunning home office is outfitted with separate workstations
for two-permanent co-workers in the main area. An auxiliary space behind the alcove on the
far wall holds a conference room to receive clients. The homeowner can access the attic from
a spiral staircase on the second floor. Clients, however, enter through the exterior staircase so
that they don't have to trample through the house. The walkout third-story porch and stairway
also provide a welcome place for the occupants to stretch their legs when they need a break.

Spanish gold interior paint and complementary grey-blue hues create a bright, cheery
environment while the walnut furniture lends a sense of seriousness that grounds the design.
Yellows are high-energy colors that brighten any room and, in this case, help to reflect light
back into the conference room behind the alcove.

The small amount of floor space a spiral staircase occupies makes it a good choice for houses that don't have room to build a traditional access to the attic or basement. However, you'll need another entrance, perhaps on the exterior of the house, that is large enough to bring in office furniture or other large items.

Whether you have a spiral or traditional staircase, look to the walls for additional storage.

Keeping your home office organized and uncluttered can make you more productive and less stressed out. Attics and basements offer innovative ways to store the things you work with most. Built-to-fit (BTF) bookcases on short and sloped walls can be functional and aesthetically appealing.

If there are high spaces you need to access regularly, consider including a library ladder in the design.

When it comes to office storage, think vertically. File cabinets form the base of every working surface, and built-in floor-to-ceiling bookcases utilize every square inch of the end wall.

Custom features help make the most of this unique attic space. The built-in work stations line opposing walls to maximize space, with plenty of cabinet storage and a divider unit that follows the ceiling slope. In addition, the custom windows offer expansive views and bring natural light into the space.

This peninsula desk frees up the wall for storage tucked behind sliding doors. The arrangement also divides this small attic space into two functional areas. Had the desk been simply pushed up against a wall, there would be a sizeable "no-man's-land" of wasted space behind the desk chair.

*Design*Wise

Peter Feinmann, founder and president
Feinmann Remodeling, Inc.
Arlington, MA

No matter how you intend to use an attic or basement, there are a few common opportunities and limitations to consider:

ATTICS

- Hot air rises; in some cases, inexpensive electric baseboard heat is all that is required to warm the space in colder months.

- Insulate with Icynene insulation to get r-factor in less space without needing the required attic ventilation. Remember to add sound insulation to the floor as well.

- The gable peaks and collar ties are ideal places for track lighting.

- To maximize the height of your attic, consider removing collar ties and adding a structural ridge beam instead.

BASEMENTS

- Don't assume that moving mechanical systems is too expensive for the amount of space that you might achieve. Removing lally columns is also possible by adding a steel channel to the existing beam instead.

- The closed cell property of Icynene insulation makes it the best choice for walls that may be exposed to moisture.

- Raise sheetrock $\frac{1}{2}$" from the floor to prevent it from absorbing moisture.

- There are a variety of interlocking plywood/rubber membrane subfloor materials available to allow for safe use of carpet, wood, and floating floor materials in most relatively dry basements. If you are carpeting your basement, use mildew-resistant synthetic padding under the carpeting or consider ceramic tile with area rugs that can be removed.

The goal for any home office is to create an efficient, compact work area where everything you need is within reach. By utilizing every nook and cranny to its fullest potential, even an attic or basement with minimal floor space can be transformed into a fully equipped office with ample elbowroom.

Built-in storage and floor-to-ceiling bookshelves keep everything neatly put away and right at your fingertips. A TV screen tucked into a corner built-in provides entertainment or access to news and financials with a spin of the task chair. And with the monitor and wires tucked under the desk hutch with a pullout drawer for the keyboard, this office manages to achieve a fairly clean, minimalist look.

*Idea*Wise

An attractive, substantial bookcase can cost $200, but you can build your own bookcase for a fraction of the cost in under an hour. To form the bookcase frame, arrange two 1" × 10" × 72" and two 1" × 10" × 36" planks on the floor and fasten with finish nails or thin wood screws.

Then cut four 1" × 10" shelves to length, place at the desired heights, and drive finish nails through the frame into the edge of each shelf. Allow a larger shelf space at the bottom for oversized books, and leave an opening at the foot of the bookcase to keep dust from accumulating.

To keep books from falling through the back of the bookcase, nail 1 × 4's horizontally across the back of each shelf space. For diagonal support, run picture-hanging wire from screws placed at each of the four corners on the back of the unit to a fifth screw placed in the middle of the back of the unit. Pull the wire taut, making sure the unit remains level.

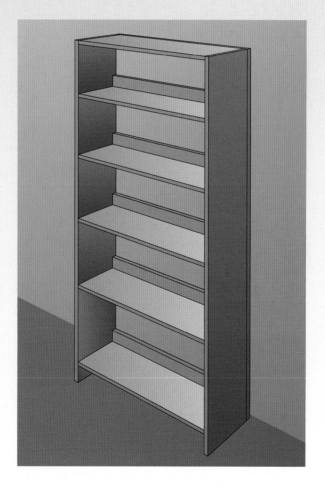

Paint is the least expensive means of transforming an unfinished attic into a pleasant living space. This otherwise small and unremarkable space is brought to life by simply painting the wood paneling with powder blue, red, and yellow.

A shallow reach-in closet and small writing surface is all the space needed for a modest home office. The entire unit can be hidden from view with a pivoting door slide; The combination slide and hinge allows the door to open 90-degrees and then slide or push back in along the inside edge of the cabinet, known as the "pocket."

A home office needn't be elaborate. If it's thoughtfully designed, even the smallest area can be an efficient workspace. Nor does a home office necessarily need its own room. In shared spaces, however, everyone will feel more comfortable if there is some sense of division or an implied boundary, such as a standing screen, curtain, bookcase, or lowered ceiling.

Basement stairways always produce a nook big enough for a small office. A simple but functional workstation can be built with a few filing cabinets, a sheet of finished plywood and a few stock or ready-to-assemble (RTA) cabinets for storage.

An open desk hutch keeps paperwork off your workspace yet readily accessible.

Bookcases can serve as protective stair railings.

A humble home office can be organized under the slope of the gable ceiling at the top of the stairs of many attics. A simple 3' × 5' rug not only saves your floor from the wear and tear caused by a rolling office chair, but it helps to define the limits of the office area.

An attic or basement that serves more than one function can be subtly divided into separate activity areas without carving up the space with walls. An exposed brick chimney provides an implied wall between this lively play space and the home office. This allows the parent to keep working while also monitoring the children's activity. Similarly, the exposed collar beams create an implied lowered ceiling which, when combined with the exposed venting pipe, defines an intimate niche within the play area itself.

Room elements like these aren't always consciously noticed, but they do influence how we feel and behave in a space. By utilizing these boundaries when designing your home office, you'll create a more comfortable workspace for yourself and help keep other family members from wandering into your space while you're hard at work.

Natural lighting can save you money. The Department of Energy reports that we spend an average of five to ten percent of our electricity bills on home lighting. This number can be as high as 25% in areas that use little air conditioning. But installing large windows, top-hinged roof windows, skylights, or sun tunnels can provide additional benefits: Rooms filled with natural light and fresh air feel more expansive and beautiful.

Keep it open

Insulating glass and low E glass help keep homes more comfortable and energy efficient.

A row of top-hinged roof windows and a large window on the gable end make this narrow office feel spacious. To provide an attic with an adequate amount of natural light, the combined area of all windows and skylights should measure at least 10 to 15 percent of the room floor space.

By installing a wall of
windows and skylights
on the southern corner of the
house where the light is
strongest, this home office takes
best advantage of the available
natural light and opens this
small workspace to the world.

*South-facing windows
and skylights capture
the maximum amount
of warmth and
natural sunlight.*

*The wire railing
provides a barrier
without interrupting
your field of vision.*

*Dollar*Wise

Opening attic windows and first floor windows creates a full house draft that can
cool your home, saving you money on air conditioning.

Good lighting is extremely important in an office, and a nice view is refreshing while working. For these reasons, home offices are usually located in attics rather than basements. But they don't have to be. With a little creativity a basement can be made into a home office every bit as comfortable as an attic.

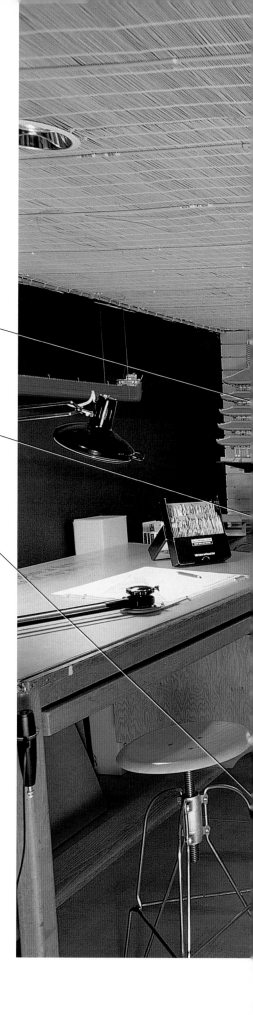

A wood or gas-burning fireplace takes the chill out of winter months.

Medium-density fiberboard (MDF) with a gray plastic laminate creates an elegant desk.

This interesting floor is created with ½" birch plywood secured to the concrete floor through ¾" rigid insulation and a vapor barrier.

Who says a basement has to be dark? A stationary window flanked by two spacious egress windows were carved out of the foundation wall, and a generously deep window well keeps natural light streaming inside.

Multiple workstations make optimum use of the available space in this converted basement. A computer station on one wall, an architect's drafting table opposite it, and a beautiful red oak filing cabinet in between them create a highly functional U-shaped desk arrangement.

Another charming aspect of the basement office is the use of untraditional materials. The beautiful ceiling is composed of matchstick reed window blinds stapled directly to the joists with an elastic cloth dust barrier in between. The house itself is a Pagoda-roofed structure; these touches from the Far East bring the exterior theme indoors. Birch veneer slat walls are an inexpensive material most often used for in-store display; however, its snap-in accessories make it useful for office storage. And rather than conceal the utilitarian features in a soffit, the hot and cold water feed-lines are simply painted with a heat-resistant paint, allowing the space to feel more open.

CHAPTER 3

Hobby Spaces

The world seems to be shrinking. In this era of the information superhighway, we're more connected than ever before. But as technology devises new and numerous ways to keep us in contact and accessible to others, it becomes more difficult to find space for ourselves to pursue our individual interests.

Even a large house can feel small if we can't find a place to be alone when we need it. Research collected by the Hobby Association shows that 58 percent of us indulge in some form of art, craft, or hobby in the home, and the number is on the rise. Part of the increasing popularity of hobbies is that they give us license to retreat into a creative world we can call our own. And what better than to carve out a dedicated space where the world of our favorite pastimes can exist.

Whether it's scrapbooking or woodworking, candle making or wine tasting, model building or oil painting, this chapter illustrates how to find the perfect space for that hobby, and why the attic or basement is a good place to look.

Many fine arts depend a great deal on controlling the quality and intensity of light in the studio to achieve the desired effect in the work. Attics tend to be brighter than basements and lend themselves to visual arts such as painting or drawing. On the other hand, the relative ease at which one can block the light from a basement lends itself to housing a photographer's dark room.

Neutral-colored walls won't compete with an artist's color palette.

Any art studio needs to have plenty of storage for supplies, good ventilation, and consistent lighting. This small attic area offers everything you need. The easel loosely defines the painting studio space against the rest of the attic. A standing screen or curtain could be installed to hide the workspace. A knee wall under the slope of a dormer provides a convenient drying nook for oversized items, and there is plenty of storage in the built-ins under the window. And most importantly, these high windows have a northern exposure, which provides the most even natural light for an art studio.

Hobbies such as photography require a variety of specialized accessories and equipment, as well as a specialized space to work: a darkroom. Basic features of darkrooms include sealed doors to prevent light from entering, a ventilation system to displace chemical fumes, a sink, lots of shelving for storage, and a "safe light" or low intensity red light that illuminates your work but will not affect photographic paper.

*Idea*Wise

Natural canvas, over-the-door shoe or-ganizers are an easy and inexpensive way to keep your studio organized. They can be purchased for under $20 at dis-count or home stores and take up virtually no studio space at all. Paint a swatch of color across each pocket so that your color palette is easy to see at a glance, and then simply hang the organizer on a nearby door or from two heavy-duty picture hang-ers on a wall. You can also use the pockets to hold brushes, sponges, pens, pencils, erasers, and other supplies.

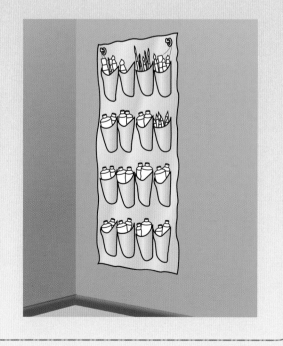

Whether you are employed as an artisan or simply enjoy spending your leisure time knitting, sewing, stenciling, scrapbooking, or making some other kind of handicraft, you are contributing to the $14 billion-a-year and growing craft industry. Many of the craft activities we take part in are easily portable, but some require spaces to spread out, space that is difficult to find on the main floors of your house. But with a little creativity and planning, you can easily transform a basement or attic into a crafter's paradise.

This A-framed attic serves as a cozy get-away for relaxing and knitting. Knitting supplies can be stored in simple wicker baskets to add accents to the space, and a chest-of-drawers can be used to store additional needles, skeins of yarn, and patterns. Additionally, craft supplies can be easily transported if you need to open up the space to guests.

Spools of thread mounted on the wall stay organized and accessible.

Sewing and quilting are activities that require space to spread out, as well as a lot of storage for the various supplies. Good lighting, smooth workspaces, and a comfortable place to sit are the prerequisites for any good sewing room. Inexpensive laminate floors provide the look of pricey redwood tongue-and-groove, and because they are perfectly smooth, it may be easier to find dropped needles. Full-spectrum overhead lighting illuminates the details, making it easier to locate seams and match up intricate fabric designs.

Attics are particularly well-suited to being music listening rooms because the angles of their walls reduce "flutter echoes" that are created in rooms with more parallel surfaces. On the other hand, the sturdy flooring of basements are naturally better as spaces for practicing music that requires heavy equipment. Both spaces are easier to insulate for sound than other rooms because they share only a floor or ceiling surface with other habitable spaces.

(above) A music listening room is separated from a home office by a striated glass wall. This gesture provides some privacy and diffused light while not closing off the space with an opaque wall. However, flat glass surfaces are a no-no in listening rooms. Use either textured glass or cover the glass surfaces with a soft cloth shade or curtain. For the same reason, the wall behind the listener should generally be absorptive (e.g., a tapestry). Reflections from the wall behind the listener reach the ears quickly and react with the direct wave from the speakers.

(left) Good listening rooms often follow the "rule of eight"—that is, your speakers should stand eight-feet apart with your listening position eight feet back, forming a triangle. While this is a good standard, be careful not to separate your speakers too wide apart for the space, as the sound may then suffer a "hole in the middle" effect.

To maintain good sound quality a listening room should contain a variety of materials so that it is neither too "hard" nor too "soft." Similarly, the ceiling and floor should be of opposite reflectivity. If the floor is absorptive (e.g., carpeting) the ceiling should be hard (e.g., drywall), and vice-versa. Also, arrange furniture, record racks, and other elements, somewhat evenly around the room to break up the sound reflections caused by parallel planes.

In the age of digital culture, where home theaters, iPods, and other electronic gadgets have taken over our lives, there is still a large and expanding part of the population that prefers reading to any other leisurely pursuit. Basement and attic libraries can serve as tranquil getaways where we have the freedom to sit down and read with all of our favorite books in one place and at our fingertips.

Stained-glass windows add a serene ambiance to any room.

Open railing made from metal cable makes this space feel more open.

Even the smallest attic space can become an elegant reading room.

A few short bookcases, a combination of sunlight and task lighting, and a comfortable chair is all that's needed for a tranquil and pleasurable reading experience.

Dictionary stands keep reference books open and readily accessible.

Libraries can provide the peace and quiet necessary for studying and practicing piano compositions. A cove or recessed ceiling is not only visually stimulating, but it is also an effective means of defining a room's space without walls. As a rule of thumb, higher ceilings tend to signify more public spaces while lower ceilings create a more intimate environment. In this basement, the soffits surrounding the cove ceiling also provide a channel for deep, recessed lighting cans.

The dark and cool environment of basements provides optimal conditions for wine storage. Cellars usually stand at a steady 55 degrees, the perfect temperature for wine which should be stored between 50-59 degrees Fahrenheit. Additionally, the relatively moderate temperature of basements prevents wine from reaching 78 degrees—the point at which it begins to uncork and "cook," resulting in a loss of quality. Humidity levels, too, should be controlled to stay between 50 and 70%. A heavy, solid-oak door helps to maintain a constant temperature and ensure that the room remains dark.

In any wine cooler intended for long-term storage, the majority of its bottles should be stored horizontally to prevent corks from drying out and oxygen from reaching the wine. Although, as in this wine cellar, you may want a display table to exhibit prized bottles of wine, as well as those you want to experience next.

A chandelier sets the mood for serious wine connoisseurs.

There's a connoisseur in all of us, and if wine or
tea is your pastime then a basement or attic is the
perfect space to accommodate your interest.

Since the 12th century, tea rituals have been performed for occasions as diverse as medicinal cleansing, meditation, guest reception, snacking, parties, and business meetings. This simple attic space has everything you need for a comfortable tearoom. Cushions provide elegant, yet inexpensive, seating. Classic bamboo shades allow tea lovers to set the lighting and mood. And a decorative standing screen creates intimacy and privacy without a permanent wall.

Because they are separate from the main floors, attics and basements are not subject to the same design constraints as the other rooms in the house, where smoothly transitioning from one space to the next tends to be more important. In these auxiliary spaces, there is the freedom to be as creative and as whimsical with the design as you like. Whether your interests lie in sailing, safari, sports, history, aviation, or botanicals, an attic or basement can provide the perfect setting for whatever dreamscape helps to transport you away from your daily cares.

*Design*Wise

Rosemary McMonigal, AIA
McMonigal Architects
Minneapolis, MN

SEWING ROOMS

- Sewing projects produce clutter, so set up space where you can manage clutter easily. If you don't have a separate room for sewing, a shared space will work fine as long as it's away from the main traffic in your home.

- Natural light is an important factor in a fully functional sewing room. Natural lighting reveals the true color balance of materials you're working with. Even "color corrected" artificial lighting isn't the same. The natural light from windows is also essential to give your eyes a break from the strain of stitching work. Finally, you will appreciate the ventilation windows afford.

WINE CELLARS

- To maintain proper humidity and temperature levels in your wine cellar, create a vapor barrier separation. Insulate the space between studs with batting, then attach sheets of 5 mil. polyethylene over the studwalls and seal the joints. You could also use rigid insulation behind studs with an open stud cavity.

(opposite) This nautical-themed room transforms an attic into a tranquil sea-faring refuge. Complete with an ocean mural, telescope, and Pullman bed with portal window, entering this space whisks us off on a romantic voyage. Tongue-and-groove hardwood maple floors can be as inexpensive as $2 to $3 per square foot and, in this case, the clear polyurethane finish completes the look of a schooner deck. Ceiling fans provide a "coastal breeze" to fight heat that rises into attics. Triangular windows suggest the sails of a ship. And stenciled paintings provide the perfect accents to complement the scene.

Ordinary rooms transformed into extraordinary dreamscapes

If you'd like to be able to park your car in your overcrowded garage, consider relocating your workshop to the basement. The nearly indestructible concrete floor can support heavy machinery and new 120V and 240V electrical service can be run from the nearby circuit breaker. In addition, basements often span the entire footprint of the first floor, providing ample workspace for even the most complex workshop.

Efficient workshops are organized in a triangle with the most important workstations at the three corners of the triangle. For instance, in this woodworking shop they are the table saw, workbench, and finishing station. Not only does this configuration make it easy to move from one phase of a project to the next, but it also helps to keep tools and materials organized. Also include an open-mouthed garbage can within easy reach for discarding wood, and rubber mats at each location to prevent muscle fatigue caused by prolonged periods of standing on hard surfaces. In addition, every workshop must be outfitted with first aid kits, smoke detectors, fire extinguishers, lockable cabinets, and phones for emergencies.

A separate entrance to a basement workshop that is at least 36" wide allows you to accommodate larger projects and materials. It also can provide added ventilation—a basement workshop should have at least two windows for cross ventilation, as well as a fan and exhaust system. To help cut down on dust, install weather-stripping on all doors. Keep a broom, dustpan and wet/dry vacuum handy as workshops accumulate sawdust that is a fire hazard, an air-quality issue, and an unpleasant material to track upstairs.

A workshop without adequate storage will go unused. Cabinets are as useful in a basement workshop as they are in the kitchen. Wall space can be used to hang light and medium-duty tools on peg-board, plywood, slat-board or a specially designed organizing system. And if you're pressed for space, consider a folding workbench that can fall flat against the wall when not in use.

Maintaining a well-labeled system of small drawers or containers for fasteners and parts will save you a lot of time fishing through buckets, and possibly save you the cost of re-purchasing what you know you already have…somewhere.

 DollarWise

One-fifth of an average house's heat escapes through its basement walls, windows and doors. Insulating your basement walls with high R-value (minimum 1-1/2" thick) mold-resistant rigid board insulation will pay for itself within a few years.

CHAPTER 4

Rec Rooms

In general, recreation rooms are spaces that can accommodate more boisterous activities than most family spaces can handle. "Rec" rooms, as they are called, are great spaces for kids to hang out and enjoy themselves with games, toys, and active play. In fact, these fun spaces give license to the kid in all of us to enjoy ourselves.

Rec rooms often begin as accidental repositories for all of the mismatched and inherited furniture and décor that just didn't look good in the rest of the house. And most often the only available space in the house for such items is found in unfinished basements and attics, where they can be tucked away from view. But rec rooms can be so much more, from game rooms to children's playrooms or home fitness centers and spas. With a little planning and forethought, a rec room can transcend its humble beginnings to become your favorite spot in the home.

Game Rooms

Game rooms are a great way to decompress and can make social gatherings more lively and spirited. A billiards or ping-pong table, air hockey, pinball, arcade games, or home video games…whatever the space will hold, go for it. Game rooms are all about fun!

Game rooms typically require a lot of space, so they are usually located in basements as opposed to attics. Basements tend to offer the larger open floor spaces desirable for most game rooms, and unlike attics, most basements already have a solid floor suitable for heavy gaming tables and roughhousing. Basements are also cooler all year round, offering a more comfortable environment for active play.

A swivel stand allows TV viewing from all areas of the room.

Staggered game tables

make the best use of space in this walkout basement. The game corner looks out to a backyard pond, creating a connection to the outdoors. The area also connects to an extended kitchen, living room, and eating area, making it part of a larger, sociable lower level.

Decorative soffit hides unsightly pipes.

Nonregulation-size pool table brings the game into a smaller space.

A rounded oak wall hides the furnace and mechanicals in this game room, allowing more space in the main area than would a straight wall. Bright sunset orange walls and matching orange felt on the pool table play off the orange undertones in the oak, and brighten what might otherwise be a small and dark basement. The wall sconces draw attention to the wall color and offer a softer light than the direct light cast from most overhead lighting. The glass block window introduces the only natural light into the room while maintaining privacy and security—a particularly good choice in a basement where capturing the view is usually undesirable. And with a laundry room nearby, you can enjoy a quick game while waiting for a load of clothes to dry.

A walkout basement can be the perfect party room for barbeques. It makes for easy access to the grill and keeps foot traffic from the outdoors out of the formal areas of the home. Bring in a pool table or other games to make the area even more fun. Comfortable seating near game tables is important as some games involve standing for long periods of time. And the nearby kitchenette is convenient for refueling between matches.

French doors lead to an outside barbecue area and allow in plenty of light.

A wine cooler keeps a fresh bottle within reach.

Cherry wood semi-custom cabinets beautify the space.

Durable, easy to maintain, man-made floors make cleanup a snap.

A small, windowless dormer with overhead spot lighting can make a cozy alcove for a game of cards. The neighboring open table with a TV makes use of the extended landing. A skylight, placed at the end of the hallway draws people into the space, and combined with the halogen track lighting, provides an energy-efficient means to flood this area with light.

A nearby half bath prevents a break in the action of the card game.

A see-through railing tricks the eye into thinking there is more floor space.

This basement game room is the ideal setting
for hosting parties or solo relaxing. The warm tone of the wood
paneling matched with the plush forest green carpeting strike the
perfect mood for a game of billiards or a cocktail at the side table.

*A billiards cue stand keeps pool sticks
organized and accessible.*

Playrooms

While playrooms are every child's dream, they can be a parent's delight as well. Converting a basement or attic into a child's play space can keep the noise and mayhem of play apart from the rest of the house.

Laminate surfaces are a great choice for playrooms because they are easy to wipe clean.

Playrooms can be adapted easily into shared spaces so that caregivers can get some work done while keeping an eye on the children. Placing a computer workstation against an attic kneewall can create more play space in the center of the room and provide a spot for the children's own projects or homework.

A few nice built-in cabinets provide perfect toy storage in a child's playroom. And with a matching custom wood cover over electric baseboard radiators, the otherwise hot mechanical is safe for children to play around or on.

It can be difficult to decide how to decorate a playroom, particularly when you know how quickly your child outgrows his or her preferences. A good way to start is to look at your child's favorite books, movies and characters and identify their favorite themes and colors. To help keep the design from falling out-date, decorate around a general theme or color scheme so as not to make the room too specific.

A desk under a skylight provides excellent natural lighting and makes any workspace feel more inviting.

*Idea*Wise

For whatever reason, children love writing on walls. Which is a problem unless they write on a surface meant to be written upon. Chalkboard paint provides just that surface. And you can make your own chalkboard paint by mixing:

3 teaspoons acrylic paint [color of choice]
1 ½ teaspoons glazing medium [water-based]
½ teaspoon powder tile grout

Apply two to three coats of paint with a regular paintbrush. Between each coat, sand the dried surface with a 400-grit or higher sandpaper, then wipe away the dust.

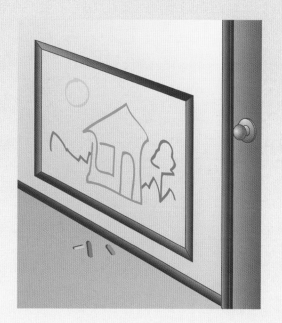

Once the last coat is dry, you need to condition your new chalkboard. Place a piece of chalk on its side and rub over the entire surface. Wipe clean with a felt cloth, and then again with a slightly damp cloth. For a finished appearance, frame the painted area with door casing.

Store children's books on low shelves that are accessible to little hands.

A place to live and learn

This child's playroom also serves as their workspace. The room is designed to be comfortable, organized, and fun so that work can be incorporated into a world of play. A good way to tie together a room that has multiple uses is to repeat each of the room's main fabrics, colors, and prints in at least three different places.

Houses are built proportionate to adult bodies, which can often leave little ones feeling disadvantaged. Inevitably, their favorite play spaces are the cozy nooks and crannies that allow them to feel completely in charge of their own environment.

This post can be removed so that large furniture can be moved up and down the stairs with ease.

An artist's painting on canvas covers a play space under the stairs. Inside the ship's galley (inset), we find a clever play space, which is also accessible from the adjoining closet.

The space under every basement staircase is perfect for a storage closet. Add a small porthole and it doubles as a favorite hideout that can draw children from all over the neighborhood.

A size-appropriate play area can be created in any room of the house. This grass green "canopy" is a camping hideaway that remains safely within earshot of the parents sleeping on the other side of the master suite.

Parents agree that toy clutter is a real problem in any room of the house, especially in the playroom. Adequate storage space in the playroom can keep the rest of your home from looking like the fallout from a toy explosion. If kids are required to put everything away before taking a nap or leaving the play area for another activity, they will grow accustom to looking for things in their place and putting them back when they belong.

This colorful basement incorporates colorful shelves and cabinets along the entire length of a wall to create an interesting backdrop for the play space, as well as plenty of storage.

Colors are vibrant, but not too child-like, so the space can grow along with the children. Hard-to-reach items are easily accessible by smaller kids by using the sturdy, built-in bench. Bins slide out for storing extra-deep items.

Stackable storage is a great way to make use of every unusually shaped nook and cranny in an attic or basement playroom. Open crates are an easy way to store toys. If it has a lid, cover or cabinet door to keep everything hidden away, so much the better.

Levelers on these roof-windows allow you to block out the light during naptime.

Windows or skylights less than 18 inches above the floor must have tempered glass.

Open shelves installed at the knee-wall below skylights and roof windows provide the perfect place to store toys, books, and bins for crayons, stickers, or markers. Label bins to help children develop organization skills.

Exercise Rooms & Spas

If you are disciplined when it comes to fitness, all you need is a resistance band, jump rope, or yoga ball for stretching and strength training. But let's face it: most of us require some kind of motivation to get in shape. The first step to treating our bodies well is to have a dedicated fitness space, and it doesn't hurt to have some kind of "reward" in the area for relaxing after a strenuous workout, such as a sauna or spa.

Important things to keep in mind when adding an exercise room or spa to your home include good lighting, adequate ventilation, and bright, cheery colors to keep you moving. And don't forget towel storage and a mini-fridge for water.

Durable, low-pile carpet or rubber mats are easy to clean and protect the floor from heavy equipment.

Studies show people tend to exercise more at home if the machines are in a specialized space and include a wide range of equipment. According to a recent survey, 29% of homeowners request a dedicated exercise room for their new home.

In small spaces, a multipurpose weight and pulley machine provides enough variety to keep exercise interesting. Using a sauna before a workout warms muscles to help lessen the possibility of injury. Prefab sauna kits are available in a variety of sizes and styles. The kits are easy to install, often times only requiring a dedicated electrical circuit.

Wainscoting echoes the Nordic white spruce wood used for the sauna.

Area rugs protect wood floor and provide a noise barrier for those below.

A flat screen TV takes up less space in an already small area.

Adequate ventilation and cooling in an attic exercise room is a must. There should be at least two operable windows so you can create a cross-breeze in the space. Check with your builder to determine if your attic floor joists can support the weight of heavy machinery.

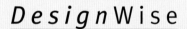

A variety of exercise equipment in a dedicated space can help you remain focused and inspired in your workout regimen. The full-wall mirrors help create the sense of more space and allow you to check on your form while exercising.

*Design*Wise

Michael Anschel
Otogawa-Anschel Creative Design-Quality Build
Minneapolis, MN

An exercise room is a place you should want to visit every day. Exercise is just as much about the mind as it is about the body:

- Avoid using cramped locations. Too small a space will feel suffocating and uninspiring.

- Finish the space with the same attention to detail that the rest of the house gets. This will help you feel like using it and keep it from becoming the space where things get dumped.

- Decorate for the activity. It should be restful and calming, allowing you to focus and let go of the day's stress. Keep out the opportunity for distractions as much as possible.

- When it comes to home spas, use a combination of natural and organic materials and shapes, with sleek manufactured products. There is nothing inviting or comfortable about a machine-edged piece of granite. A curve that is not calculated, but rather drawn by hand will fit the space far better.

Relaxation is as important to a healthy lifestyle as is exercise. Stress is supposed to be a short-term response to a crisis that demands an immediate response. For many of us, however, that feeling has turned into a way of life. The effects can be very detrimental to our health. During a period of stress, or crisis, blood pressure rises, the immune system is depressed, fat metabolism is inhibited, we're more easily fatigued, and we're more prone to depression.

Pampering yourself with a home spa can provide much-needed renewal for your mind, body, and soul. Larger showers and whirlpool bathtubs, saunas, and lounging areas are essential elements that can transform ordinary bathrooms into relaxing retreats.

Natural materials and neutral colors contribute to the peaceful environment of a home spa. A teak wood sink-surround creates a warm and inviting vanity area and built-in speakers provide soothing music to help shut out the busy world.

A luxury shower with multiple handles and a glass door encourages a relaxing bathing ritual. A whirlpool bathtub ensures that bathing is not just cleansing, but therapeutic as well—a fact not lost on many as: 58% of people building new homes request a whirlpool bath in the master suite.

A Mandi bathing bowl is inspired by those used in Indonesia, where quick "splash washing" is customary (and conserves water).

Saunas originated as a social center for bringing family and friends together, but they can also provide a private sanctuary for relaxation and renewal. In
this spacious shower and sauna area, a glass door on the sauna and a shared cedar
plank ceiling link the two spaces. An open, glass-block wall allows quick movement
between the warmth of a sauna and a cool-down shower and resting area.

Use stretching machines while muscles are still warm to reduce the possibility of injury.

Tile flooring is impervious to the excess moisture native to this space.

Steam rooms fit into the same amount of space as a standard tub or shower

and provide humid heat as an alternative to the dry air of the sauna. Both saunas and steam rooms may relax stiff joints and muscles, cleanse your skin, eliminate toxins, raise your metabolism, and boost your immune system. Additionally, steam inhalation is an effective treatment in respiratory conditions, and through the use of essential oils in your steam spa's delivery system, you can pursue the benefits of aromatherapy, as well.

CHAPTER 5

Bedrooms

Though we don't give it much thought, we spend as much as a third of our lives in our bedrooms. That's a lot of time. So it's well worth our while to create a bedroom environment that is comfortable and uniquely our own. Not only will we appreciate our homes more, we will be more likely to get the rest needed to tackle the other two-thirds of our lives.

A bedroom is a highly personal space. What makes a bedroom perfect for one person may not make it so for another. All great bedrooms, however, are alike in that they are designed to be retreats from the outside world. Ideally, they are in close proximity to a full bath, offer storage to keep the room uncluttered, are decorated with soothing colors, and include pleasant memorabilia associated with happy memories.

Whether you're considering a guest room, an additional bedroom for the kids or a full master suite, basements and attics are the ideal location for a bedroom. Both spaces are set apart from the main living areas, so retiring for the night creates the sense that we are leaving our everyday cares behind, making it easier to relax, wind down, and get some rest.

For those of you blessed with a large attic, you can transform the space into a luxurious master suite complete with a bedroom, bathroom, and sitting area. The national average for a remodel of that magnitude is approximately $70,000; however, just over 80% of those costs are recouped at resale. The recoup value is even higher for more modest attic bedrooms.

This master bedroom suite feels bright and open while remaining cozy. A vaulted ceiling like this one can be dramatic, but its imposing height can also make us feel small and exposed. For that reason, vaulted ceilings tend to be more appropriate in larger public spaces.

To combat the steep pitch of the ceiling in this bedroom, the exposed collar beams imply a lowered ceiling that defines the private space of the bedroom without losing the sense of openness provided by the vaulted ceiling.

The matching built-in cabinets and knee wall serve the dual purpose of hiding ductwork and providing storage. The lounge chairs and area rug are organized around a wood-burning fireplace, creating a cozy sitting area. This was a great design choice. Establishing two different functions for one room make the space feel much larger, and the fireplace adds instant value to a home, 13% at resale on average.

This attic achieves its sense of openness and sophistication by leaving everything from railing and plumbing to bricks and beams exposed. The built-in bookcases act as media storage, a safety rail and an elegant see-through wall.

Exposed brick can be a stylish accent in any room. Here it serves as an innovative backsplash for a bathroom vanity. Copper pipes are highlighted rather than hidden, contributing to the room's charm.

Sleeping areas require a hard-wired smoke detector but should have a carbon monoxide detector as well.

Attics and basements are oftentimes smaller than the main floors. Even if they do have the same footprint as the main levels, the sloped ceilings of attics and scarcity of natural light in basements make them feel small regardless of their size. So, closing off these spaces further is the last thing you want to do. In the next few pages we'll examine a few creative ways to partition space in an attic or basement without the use of full walls.

In this small master suite bathroom, locating the toilet under the roof slope freed-up the open ceiling space for the shower and vanity area. The all-glass shower helps enlarges the space by not restricting the view with solid walls. The tub's painted exterior is a lively modern twist to the traditionally white claw-foot tub.

Subway tile is the common name for 2" × 6" wall tile laid in a brick pattern. A common feature in bungalows in the first half of the century, today subway tile is seeing a resurgence in popularity, partly because the staggered brick pattern is more forgiving than straight-line tile patterns on crooked walls.

One way to carve a sleeping space from a larger room is with a room divider. This internally lit screen allows light to filter through and provides a bright, clean look. A Japanese screen or room divider can turn any area into two functional spaces while still allowing your attic or basement to feel airy and open.

Layering: a trick of perspective.

Transform your attic simply by applying bright paints to pre-existing paneling.

Light from a window or fixture at the end of a hallway draws people into a space.

This small attic has made great use of a limited space. There are no full walls to obstruct our view, but our eyes recognize two distinct layers: the narrow hallway in the foreground and the reading alcove beyond it. The green knee wall suggests where one space ends and the next begins. And when there are two or more layers in our field of vision, we perceive depth that may not actually exist, causing each space to appear larger than it actually is.

A platform bed sits low to the floor and doesn't require a box-spring, helping this small bedroom to feel larger. In fact, a platform bed may be your only option—in an old house with a narrow attic stairway, it may be impossible to move a rigid box-spring up the stairs.

*Design*Wise

Michael Anschel
Otogawa-Anschel Creative Design-Quality Build
Minneapolis, MN

- Wall sconces. I can't say enough about them. Up light (like lamps) is generally more pleasing to be around, and is far more forgiving to your space. There are so many colors and styles out there right now; you can really alter the mood and look of a room with the right fixtures.

- You can use color to force a space to retain its 3-D nature even when light threatens to flatten it out. Applying variated shades of a color to the different planes as you move through the room, you will create what I call "Permanent Shadow." This is especially useful when working with colors on the extremes of light and dark.

- If you can't add walls, draw the lines on the floor and on the walls. Change your flooring material or wall colors to create 'invisible' walls that guide you through the space and keep things in their proper place.

- Bamboo and palm floors are another great area to spend a little extra. They look great, they are comfortable to stand on, durable, and more importantly not a 'fad' item like Cork or Corian. On top of it all, they are "green" products.

Making more with less

Using a few simple design principles, this narrow room (scarcely 8 feet wide), feels open and spacious. A narrow partition wall provides privacy by splitting the bedroom into sitting and sleeping areas. The floor space may be minimal, but the tall ceiling is an asset. To make the most of the expansive vaulted ceiling, the vertical lines in the pine wall and knee wall, along with the stationary half-round window and complementary mirror, lead the eye upwards, making the room feel less "boxy." And the bright custard yellow opens the room by maximizing the glow of natural light.

Wall mounted swing light fixture keeps tabletops clear.

Because darker colors feel "closer" than lighter colors, the sun-
flower yellow on the gable wall exaggerates the length of the room when juxtaposed
with the poppy red of the ceilings. The rug runner contributes to the effect.

Combined with a periwinkle blue that is used in other areas of this bedroom
suite, these colors are a "triadic" relation—three equally spaced colors on the color-
wheel that provide a rich but harmonious visual contrast. The skylight opposite the
bed offers additional natural light to make the colors stand out during the day and
provides a view of the sky at night.

For a toned-down version of this design, choose a stand-out color for the headboard
wall and paint the other three walls with a complementary, relaxing, warm color.

*Red paint is continued on the
end wall, altering the precieved
depth of the tight corner.*

Three asymmetrically placed 'windows' allow air to circulate throughout the attic suite.

Strong colors applied with confidence and vivid imagination can make some people swear off of white walls for good. In this attic, a bouquet of rich, deep colors—periwinkle blue, apple green, sunset orange, and butter yellow—treat the eye to a tour around the color wheel. Even the flooring is incorporated into the inventive use of angles and colors: here Brazilian cherry and birch flooring are used to distinguish between the sitting area and bedroom.

With one sightline spanning the entire length of this space, the attic feels more spacious. The dramatic angles of the two openings into the bedroom inform you that you've entered a new place without the hindrance of doors.

Having a bathing area and washing basin in a bedroom makes the morning or evening bathing ritual more convenient. You'll be surprised how nice it is to not have to bump into anyone in the hallway when you're half asleep. Tiling the tub surround and backsplash with an attractive mix of rusts, greens, and gold, makes this room one-of-a-kind.

This pocket door is a reclaimed swing door to match the other doors in the house.

Pocket doors are advantageous because they do not take up floor space like swing doors. However, they need a wide wall cavity into which to slide. To make room for this pocket door, the door opening had to be moved tightly into the corner. To make the space appear less cramped, the lavender wedge following the slope of the ceiling creates the illusion of more space around the closet.

A master bedroom in an attic or basement is always more comfortable when the master bath is located on the same floor. While installing a new bath can be a big project, it always pays off: the addition of a full bath adds about 24% to the resale value of your home.

In some attics, the original floor structure may not be up to building code requirement for a finished space with a full tub. In that case, 2 × 10s must be installed between the old joists, often 2 × 6s, to reinforce the floor. And as with any attic bathroom, new plumbing waste pipes and vent pipes cannot simply be merged with those from the lower level; new pipes have to be installed to avoid creating a vacuum in the system.

A bath doesn't necessarily have to be tucked away in a corner. This contemporary master bath suite is located near the center of the attic and the bedroom occupies the cozy dormer behind it. A staggered wall offers privacy to those in either space without closing off the entry area. Raspberry accent tile dramatically sets off the bathtub from the vertical grain bamboo tub surround.

A wall sconce provides a diffuse light to read by while bathing.

In this sleek contemporary bathroom, every effort is made to allow unimpeded movement and open sightlines. The open window above the chrome and glass shower allows in additional natural light, makes the space feel less confined, and keeps moisture from getting trapped in the shower box. The sink and thin vanity shelf complement each other in shape, color, and design, helping to pull together the minimalist theme.

A separate water closet is a popular feature for added privacy in a master bath.

Bamboo flooring is naturally water-resistant and a beautiful addition to any master bathroom.

When transforming your basement or attic into a bedroom, it is important to consider what storage will best suit your needs. Keep in mind that clothes closets must be a minimum of 3-ft. wide × 2-ft. deep.

Oftentimes closets feel like the most disorderly places in our homes, usually because we don't have enough room to put everything in a designated place. A custom built-in closet system holds 50-75% more than the traditional one-rail closet. The best closet designs are customized for exactly the things you have, and make use of every square inch of available space.

A closet window allows you to enjoy the daylight each morning while getting dressed.

This built-in wardrobe efficiently and beautifully utilizes sloped wall space that a free-standing dresser could not take advantage of.

This clever built-in tucked into an attic knee wall can be removed to reveal additional hidden storage and allow access to mechanicals.

*Idea*Wise

If you're looking for more closet space but don't have room to build, consider installing a "flying closet." Simply purchase a decorative hanging pot rack or set of closet rods. Secure eye-hooks with ¼" thread diameter to the ceiling joists in a corner of the room and hang the flying closet from them with a medium density chain. Use a folding shade or screen to conceal the closet or to create a dressing area.

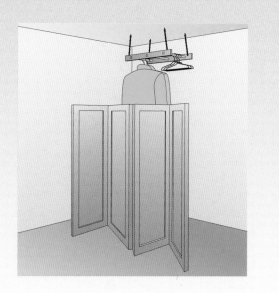

Nearly any unused attic space can be transformed into a cozy bedroom suite complete with bathroom and storage areas tucked into trickier spaces.

In this bedroom, a window is placed on the left third of the wall.

Asymmetrical accents that divide a space into thirds or fifths tend to be more playful and interesting than perfectly symmetrical details. In this case the off-center window not only brings some light into the area, but it is a focal point on that side of the room. More importantly, it was less expensive to install than a larger window! The egress bay window on the left brings extra light into the space.

Every effort is made to make the most of this small space. Shorter items like a dresser and a crib fit neatly under sloped ceilings. Instead of cluttering the space with a bedside table and lamp, an overhead light is installed for nighttime reading. The smooth surfaces of these solid oak hardwood floors make a space feel larger than the textured surfaces of wall-to-wall carpeting. A throw rug, though, is the difference between a minimalist look and a barren appearance.

A skylight can be made to feel more like a window by installing a "windowsill" where the sloped wall meets a flat wall. It also adds depth and creates extra storage space for this small bathroom. A bright, strong accent color, like this periwinkle, livens up a small room.

Tile floor is water resistant and easy to clean.

The right fireplace can transform a small attic bedroom into a cozy and romantic space. Here, a decorative copper hood adds a sense of height to a small room. A direct-vent fireplace can be installed easily in any attic.

The basic rectangular unit is the building block of almost all window styles, but this impressive gable wall window system is composed of a central pentoid casement window surrounded by custom stationary windows. In this way, the window system is able to conform to the triangular shape of the end wall and maximize the amount of light brought into the space—making even a small bedroom feel expansive.

As a general rule of thumb, the total area of window space in a room should add up to no less than ten to fifteen percent of the total floor space. Natural light from the east or southeast is especially important in a bedroom, where the mood for the day is set upon waking.

Zoning regulations require a minimum of 5.7 square feet of open area in a bedroom egress window, with the clear opening dimension of no less than 24 inches high and 20 inches wide. For accessibility, the sill height must not be more than 44 inches above the floor.

Traditional double-hung windows have a classic look, but only open halfway. This unique fully-functional double-hung window also opens inward to serve as sufficient egress.

Electric baseboard heaters take up less room and are less expensive to install than a radiator.

*Dollar*Wise

Every attic or basement bedroom needs an egress window. Casement windows are the least expensive option because the entire frame is a clear opening. In contrast, double-hung and sliding windows only open half-way. To offer the same size clear opening as a casement window, they would have to be twice as big, and therefore almost twice as expensive.

A basement bedroom doesn't have to feel like it's in a basement. This elegant, inviting space draws from a Victorian theme. Though the bed blocks the window, the effect is stunning: the open headboard lets light through to highlight the elegant floral pattern scrollwork.

Ideally, the bed should be placed in a position where the occupants can see anyone entering the room. This provides a subconscious sense of security, putting the mind at ease before drifting into dream.

An area rug is a decorative element that can add warmth to any bedroom.

A contemporary bedroom setting with a metal headboard, simple bedspread, and clean design is softened by the addition of antique nightstands, traditional lighting, an Oriental rug, and a striped window valance. These traditional touches add texture to the otherwise sleek modern design.

Attics and basements are perfect spaces for creating a guest bedroom for oc-
casional visitors. Guest bedrooms don't have to be expensively furnished; just
the necessities will do. Start with a comfortable bed or two and some storage
area for clothes. Decorative touches can always be added over time.

*Clever design: One shelf bracket points up
and out of the way, while the other points
down to accommodate the roof slope.*

An attic bedroom with beds that resemble train berths is perfect for a
visiting family. Separating beds with partition walls is an inexpensive way to
gives both kids and parents some privacy. Natural light from a skylight and a
double-hung window makes it easier to rouse kids in the morning.

Murphy beds, or wall beds, are stored vertically inside a wall cabinet or cavity and fold downward when needed. They use specially designed mattresses weighted for the spring-balanced Murphy frame and, when stored vertically, occupy as little as 16-in. of floor space. Initial installation of many models takes from 4 to 6 hours to complete, and most manufacturers recommend that they be professionally installed. They are perfect for rooms with limited space.

Kids' rooms are the places where decorating and furniture choices can be as whimsical or fantastical as a parent can endure. What better place for an adventuresome kid's room than out of the way in an attic or a basement.

A "Secret Garden"-themed bedroom can "bring the outside in" to an otherwise closed-in basement. Clever and efficient use of gardening materials gives this room a playful feel. The white picket fence painted on the wall creates the sense of an outdoors within reach. Similarly, the shutters mounted to the wall help make the room feel open despite the lack of windows. A combination of fresh and imitation plants and flowers complete the fun theme.

A decorative birdhouse mounted on a measuring stick allows children to measure their height during growth spurt years.

A room does not have to be small to justify a loft bed. In any room, the structure dramatically increases storage space. And kids love them because they provide additional play area. A playful rug and some fun pillows placed on the floor beneath a loft is an easy way to make a cozy reading area for kids.

Lining the walls of a child's bedroom with cabinets allows for toy and clothing storage that the child can access themselves. Use higher cabinets for inactive storage.

Kids can hang their "master-pieces" from a mounted bar with hooks without damaging walls.

With a little creativity, the awkward angles and recess of an attic can be the biggest asset in creating fun kids' bedrooms.

In this aeronautically themed kid's bedroom, triangular shapes and angled lines dominate. They show up in rug patterns, window valances, and shelving built-ins. Mounted on the sloped walls, the mirrors produce a fun-house effect. And the sloped display shelving and platform bed of this biplane fit perfectly under the slope of the attic wall.

CHAPTER 6

In-Law Suites

A s the population ages, more and more families are looking for affordable alternatives to high-priced assisted-living facilities. An in-law suite, a second self-contained living quarter in a single-family home, is becoming an increasingly common solution.

Also called "second suites," "accessory apartments," or "granny flats," in-law suites are often subject to zoning bylaws designed to curtail their use as retail rentals for nonfamily members. Some jurisdictions prohibit a single-family home from having two full kitchens, while others forbid a suite from having a separate entrance. However, in many areas, bylaws are changing to accommodate the growing desire for extended families to live together under one roof. These jurisdictions may simply require that there is a direct access from the main dwelling to the in-law suite and may periodically ask for verification that there is a family member living in the space.

Zoning issues aside, a basement or attic is the ideal location for an in-law suite. Because they are apart of the house structure, and yet set apart from the main living area, these spaces strike the perfect balance between the occupant's need for independence and for close contact with the family when desired.

Handicap accessibility, or "universal design," can be an important consideration for an in-law suite. Walkout basements are perfect places for these self-contained apartments because these single-floor settings allow for greater mobility indoors as well as accessibility to the outdoors. If your in-law suite is not on the ground level, you can install a handicap-accessible ramp for wheelchair and walker access to the house if necessary. For more information regarding universal design, contact the National Kitchen and Bath Association (www.nkba.com).

Large pass-throughs to the living area and to a small but fully functional kitchenette allow the occupant greater independence. These considerations may not be important to short-term guests, but for a full-time aging relative, they are critical in fostering a relationship of equality and respect.

Multiple diversions make this a comfortable and fun living space. The seating area is grouped around the flat screen television and fireplace, but the TV can also be viewed from the card table, the pool table, and the kitchenette.

*Idea*Wise

In small kitchenettes, you need every inch of counter space. Instead of allowing your wire dish rack to clutter the sink area, mount it on the wall above your sink. Rest the top rim of the dish rack on two screws with oversized heads and secure tightly to the wall. Then place an eye-hook above and to the outside of each screw. If there isn't a wall stud to fasten to, be sure to use plaster mollies. Then simply run a thin chain from each eyehook to the front corners of the dish rack.

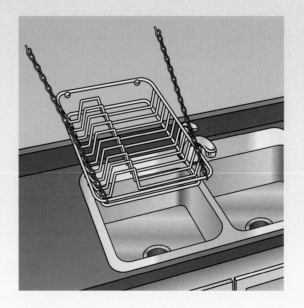

(above) Looking out from the cherry wood kitchenette, the molded ceiling and wooden beams add a touch of elegance to this lower level that is usually reserved for upper floors. While a Tudor-style light fixture and antique furnishings echo this formal look, curved arches in the doorway and bookshelves lend a softer feel to a room also used for recreational purposes.

(right) A storage wall adds visual depth to a space and gives live-in family members a place to put objects brought from their homes that are important to them.

This bath features a wheelchair accessible shower and a handicap-accessible toilet with grab-bar.

*Design*Wise

Robert Gerloff, AIA
Robert Gerloff Residential Architects
Minneapolis, MN

- Soundproof the walls and floors between your in-law suite and your home as much as possible. Use sound insulation in the walls, install solid-core rather than hollow-core doors, and if possible, install the sheetrock on "sound channels."

- Plan for future health concerns. Slightly wider doors (2-ft. 10-in. in residences are fine) and larger bathrooms allow more space for maneuvering walkers or wheelchairs. Additionally, low-barrier shower units and grab-bars around elongated toilets will extend the time your in-laws can stay in the unit.

- Design in a kitchenette if at all possible, even if it's only a microwave and a refrigerator.

Your in-laws will feel more independent if they can make their own coffee and breakfast in the morning without having to come into the main kitchen.

- Install a separate entrance to the in-law suite if at all possible so your in-laws can have their privacy, their guests can come and go without disturbing your family, and so everyone can feel more independent.

- Provide windows to the street if at all possible. Privacy and views to nature are fine, but human beings are social creatures and love to see who's coming and going.

- Above all, plan now for how the in-law space could be used in the future. Can it be converted into a master bedroom suite? Would it function well as a home office? Could it be rented out as an apartment?

In-law suites can be an ideal arrangement for an extended family, but they may also provide desirable lodging for live-in babysitters, health care workers, guests, other family members that may visit for extended periods of time, or even to give a teenager a measured taste of independence.

This plush, Tuscan-inspired in-law suite was designed for young adults visiting from school. There is a home theater and bar with tasting table to use for entertaining guests as well.

Rather than lining up furniture along the walls, "floating furnishings" in the middle of the room into close-knit groupings no more than 8 feet apart routes traffic around a sitting area rather than through it to create intimate conversation areas for family or guests.

A gently curved stairway adorned with copper pots and faux walls made to look like aged-plaster provide a beautiful transition to and from the basement. If necessary, a motorized chair lift could make this accessible to everyone.

An attractive, solid oak dining room table with a serving buffet is a great place to entertain or to bring the extended family together for a meal.

This sensible Arts and Crafts style attic space provides a casual area for children to do homework, relax, or entertain friends. Self-contained with a kitchenette, dining area, and bedroom, it can also serve as an in-law suite.

A kitchenette with microwave and sink allows children to make themselves quick snacks but not large messy meals.

Dormers can provide the added space needed to create the per-fect nook. Here, a thick leather couch, flatscreen TV, and plenty of natural light from a transom window make this an inviting area for hanging out. Directly behind the couch, a desk takes advantage of the remain-ing space, providing a perch for doing homework or paying bills.

Resource Guide

A listing of resources for information, designs, and products found in IdeaWise Basements & Attics.

Introduction

page 3 (bottom left)
skylights by
VELUX-America, Inc.
800-88-velux
www.veluxUSA.com

page 3 (bottom right)
basement by
Tea 2 Architects
612-929-2800
www.tea2architects.com

page 8
skylights by
VELUX-America, Inc.
800-88-velux
www.veluxUSA.com

page 10
billiards by
Cal Spas
800-CAL-SPAS
www.calspas.com

Family Spaces

pages 14-15 (both)
basement by
Rehkamp Larson Architects, Inc.
612-285-7275
www.rehkamplarson.com

pages 16-17
basement by
Tea 2 Architects
612-929-2800
www.tea2architects.com

pages 18-19 (both)
basement designs by
Gayle Jagoda
Schloegel Design Remodel, Inc.
816-361-9669
www.RemodelAgain.com

pages 20-21 (all)
attic design by
Tea 2 Architects
612-929-2800
www.tea2architects.com

pages 22-23
skylights by
VELUX-America, Inc.
800-88-velux
www.veluxUSA.com

page 24
basement bar by
Newland Architecture
Minneapolis, Minnesota
612-926-2424
www.newlandarchitecture.com

pages 26-29 (all)
basement designs by
Robert Gerloff Residential Architecture
Minneapolis, Minnesota
612-927-5913

page 34 (bottom)
pleated shades by
VELUX-America, Inc.
800-88-velux
www.veluxUSA.com

page 35 (top)
under bed storage by
Room and Board
800-486-6554
www.roomandboard.com

page 35 (bottom)
DesignWise by
Jake Schloegel, president
Schloegel Design Remodel, Inc.
Kansas City, Missouri
816-361-9669
www.RemodelAgain.com

page 36-37 (both)
home theater by
William Beson Design
Minneapolis, Minnesota
612-338-8187
www.williambeson.com

Home Offices

page 38
skylights by
VELUX-America, Inc.
800-88-velux
www.veluxUSA.com

page 47
office design (top)
DesignWise by
Peter Feinmann
Feinmann Remodeling, Inc.
781-643-6269
www.feinmann.com

page 48
skylights by
VELUX-America, Inc.
800-88-velux
www.veluxUSA.com

page 50 (top)
attic design by
Otogawa-Anschel Design & Build
Minneapolis, Minnesota
612-789-7070
www.otogawa-anschel.com

page 51
home office by
California Closets
800-274-6754
www.calclosets.com

pages 52-53 (both)
attic design by
Robert Gerloff Residential Architecture
Minneapolis, Minnesota
612-927-5913

page 54
skylights by
VELUX-America, Inc.
800-88-velux
www.veluxUSA.com

pages 56-57
basement office by
Newland Architecture
Minneapolis, Minnesota
612-926-2424
www.newlandarchitecture.com

Resource Guide

(continued)

Hobby Spaces

page 59
attic windows by
Andersen Windows and Doors
888-888-7020
www.andersenwindows.com

page 60
attic design by
Robert Gerloff Residential Architecture
Minneapolis, Minnesota
612-927-5913

page 61
basement darkroom by
Feinmann Remodeling, Inc.
781-643-6269
www.feinmann.com

page 63
attic design by
Awad & Koontz Architect Builders Inc.

pages 67-68 (both)
basement designs by
Tea 2 Architects
612-929-2800
www.tea2architects.com

page 69
attic flooring by
BR-111™
800-525-2711
www.br111.com

page 71
DesignWise by
Rosemary McMonigal, AIA
McMonigal Architects
Minneapolis, Minnesota
612-331-1244

pages 72-73 (all)
basement workshop by
**Dave Vincent at
Binkey's Woodworking**
www.binkeyswoodworking.com

Rec Rooms

Resource Guide
(continued)

Bedrooms

Page 100-101 (all)
attic design by
LOCUS Architecture, Ltd.
612-706-5600
www.locusarchitecture.com

page 102
attic bath by
David Heidi Design
Minneapolis, Minnesota
612-337-5060

page 103
furnishings by
IKEA
800-434-4532
www.IKEA.com

page 104-105 (all)
attic designs and DesignWise by
Michael Anschel
Otogawa-Anschel Design & Build
Minneapolis, Minnesota
612-789-7070
www.otogawa-anschel.com

page 107-111 (all)
attic designs by
Otogawa-Anschel Design & Build
Minneapolis, Minnesota
612-789-7070
www.otogawa-anschel.com

page 112 (top)
attic closet by
California Closets
800-274-6754
www.calclosets.com

page 112 (bottom)
attic bath by
David Heidi Design
Minneapolis, Minnesota
612-337-5060

page 113
attic built-in by
Mindy Sloo, Architect
Minneapolis, Minnesota
612-870-7098

pages 114-115 (both)
attic designs by
Otogawa-Anschel Design & Build
Minneapolis, Minnesota
612-789-7070
www.otogawa-anschel.com

page 117 (both)
attic design by
Mindy Sloo, Architect
Minneapolis, Minnesota
612-870-7098

pages 118-119 (both)
basement bedrooms by
David Heidi Design
Minneapolis, Minnesota
612-337-5060

page 121 (both)
attic design by
Quigley Architects
Minneapolis, Minnesota
612-692-8850

page 123 (top)
furnishings by
IKEA
800-434-4532
www.IKEA.com

In-law Suites

pages 126-128 (all)
basement design by
David Heidi Design
Minneapolis, Minnesota
612-337-5060

page 129
DesignWise by
Robert Gerloff Residential Architecture
Minneapolis, Minnesota
612-927-5913

page 130-131 (all)
basement design by
William Beson Interior Design
Minneapolis, Minnesota
612-337-5060
www.williambeson.com

page 132-133 (both)
attic design by
David Heidi Design
Minneapolis, Minnesota
612-337-5060

Photo Credits

Front cover photo and title page: ©David Livingston/ www.davidduncanlivingston.com.

BackCover: (top left) ©Brand X Pictures; (top right) Photo courtesy of The Company Store; (center) Photo courtesy of Schloegel Design Remodel, Inc./www.remodelagain.com; (bottom left) Photo courtesy of Room and Board; (bottom right) ©David Carmack Photography, Boston for Feinmann Remodeling, Inc.

p. 2: ©Brand X Pictures.

p. 3: (bottom left) Photo courtesy of VELUX-America; (bottom right) ©Andrea Rugg for Tea 2 Architects.

p. 4: ©Brian Vanden Brink.

p. 7: (top) ©Jeff Krueger for Crystal Cabinets; (bottom) ©Brian Vanden Brink for John Libby, Barnmasters.

p. 8: Photo courtesy of VELUX-America.

p. 9: ©Andrea Rugg for Locus Architecture, Cabinets by Thompson Woodworks and Mfg. Co.

p. 10: Photo courtesy of Cal Spas.

p. 12: ©Karen Melvin for LEK Design Group, Inc.

pp. 14-15: (both) ©Andrea Rugg for Rehkamp Larson Architects, Inc.

pp. 16-17: (both) ©Andrea Rugg for Tea 2 Architects.

pp. 18-19: (both) Photos courtesy of Schloegel Design Remodel, Inc./www.remodelagain.com.

pp. 20-21: (all) ©Andrea Rugg for Tea 2 Architects.

pp. 22-23: Photo courtesy of VELUX-America.

p. 24: ©Andrea Rugg for Newland Architecture.

pp. 26-29: (all) ©Andrea Rugg for Robert Gerloff Residential Architects.

pp. 30-31: ©David Livingston/www.davidduncanliv-ingston.com.

pp. 32-33: ©Brian Vanden Brink for Custom Electronics.

p. 34: (top) ©Arcaid/Alamy; (bottom) Photo courtesy of VELUX-America.

p. 35: Photo courtesy of Room and Board.

pp. 36-37: ©Andrea Rugg for William Beson Design.

p. 38: Photo courtesy of VELUX-America.

pp. 40-41: ©Brian Vanden Brink for Chris Glass, Architect.

pp.42-43: (both) ©Andrea Rugg-photography on walls by Brian Scott Holman.

p. 44: ©IML Image Group, Ltd./Alamy.

p. 45: ©Brand X Pictures.

p. 46 (left): ©Beateworks, Inc./Alamy; (right) ©Karen Melvin.

p. 47: ©David Carmack Photography, Boston for Feinmann Remodeling, Inc.

p. 48: Photo courtesy of VELUX-America.

p. 50: (top)©Andrea Rugg for Otogawa-Anschel Design and Build; (bottom) ©Beateworks, Inc./Alamy.

p. 51: Photo courtesy of California Closets.

pp. 52-53: (both) ©Andrea Rugg for Robert Gerloff Residential Architects.

p. 54: Photo courtesy of VELUX-America.

p. 55: Elizabeth Whiting & Associates/Alamy.

pp. 56-57: ©Andrea Rugg for Newland Architecture.

p. 58: Photo courtesy of Andersen Windows and Doors.

p. 60: ©Andrea Rugg for Tea 2 Architects.

p.61: ©David Carmack Photography, Boston for Feinmann Remodeling, Inc.

p. 62: ©Brian Vanden Brink.

p. 63: ©Andrea Rugg for Awad & Koontz Architects Builders, Inc.

pp. 64-65: (both) ©Andrea Rugg.

p. 66: ©Brian Vanden Brink for John Libby, Barnmasters.

Index